To Marie Ardern, Lesley Olley, Colin Bell:
Grand Supporters

— D.H.

Dedicated to the indomitable Niki Ward,
and her son Master Björn

— P.M.

PUFFIN

UK | USA | Canada | Ireland | Australia
India | New Zealand | South Africa | China

Puffin is an imprint of the Penguin Random House group of companies,
whose addresses can be found at global.penguinrandomhouse.com.

Penguin
Random House
New Zealand

First published by Penguin Random House New Zealand, 2020

3 5 7 9 10 8 6 4 2

Text © David Hill, 2020
Illustrations © Phoebe Morris, 2020

Design by Cat Taylor © Penguin Random House New Zealand
Prepress by Image Centre Group
Printed and bound in China by RR Donnelley

A catalogue record for this book is available from the
National Library of New Zealand.

ISBN 978-0-14-377451-8

penguin.co.nz

MIX
Paper from
responsible sources
FSC® C144853
FSC
www.fsc.org

TAKING THE LEAD

How Jacinda Ardern Wowed the World

WRITTEN BY
DAVID HILL

ILLUSTRATED BY
PHOEBE MORRIS

PUFFIN

In a Waikato orchard, a teenage girl has her first driving lesson. It isn't an ordinary lesson; she's driving a tractor.

And this isn't an ordinary girl. She's already going places. One day, she will be New Zealand's Prime Minister.

Jacinda Ardern was born in Hamilton, in 1980. The family moved to the forestry town of Murupara, where her father Ross was a policeman.

Murupara had some poor families. Jacinda's schoolmates sometimes had no shoes and no lunch. She wanted to do something about this.

By the time she started high school, the Arderns had moved to Morrinsville. Her mother Laurell ran the canteen at the town's high school.

Jacinda loved their orchard. She learned to drive there. Players on a nearby golf course accidentally hit balls into the orchard, and Jacinda sold them back.

$2

20c

When Jacinda was little, she had wanted to be a clown. Now she wondered whether to become a scientist, as her elder sister Louise would do, or go into politics.

Some kids laughed at her for wanting to help people so much. But that didn't stop Jacinda. She just got on with it.

Two things helped her choose politics. For a school project, she spoke to Marilyn Waring, who had been a local Member of Parliament. Jacinda was impressed by how friendly and helpful Ms Waring was.

Soon after that, Jacinda's Auntie Marie invited her to come to New Plymouth, and work for the Labour Party in the 1999 General Election.

Here was a real chance to help people. So Jacinda took time off from her after-school supermarket job. She drove to New Plymouth in her little old car, and learned how to organise meetings and election events.

She had lots more places to go after that. She studied at Waikato University, then worked in Wellington for the Labour Party. Helen Clark had become New Zealand's second female Prime Minister, and needed people to help with research. So Jacinda got on with that, too.

Next, she travelled overseas. She worked at a New York soup kitchen, serving food to poor and homeless people.

In England, she joined the cabinet office of British Prime Minister Tony Blair. She also joined the International Union of Socialist Youth. This group worked for human rights, and for equal opportunities for the world's children.

Jacinda was soon chosen as the Union's President. She travelled to meetings in China, Lebanon, Jordan, and other countries. The young New Zealander was certainly going places.

In 2008, when Jacinda was 28, she returned to New Zealand and was elected to Parliament as the country's youngest MP. Her first speech called for all children to learn te reo Māori at school, and for action against climate change.

Newspaper and TV commentators sometimes said that Jacinda was only a pretty young woman. They felt she wasn't tough enough or experienced enough to be a good politician. She didn't let this put her off her work. She just got on with it.

Jacinda Ardern wasn't only busy with politics.

She performed as a DJ at an Auckland festival and in record shops. Her playlist included the Beatles and her favourite New Zealand bands.

She met Clarke Gayford, a keen fisherman from Gisborne and a TV and radio host. Jacinda enjoys fishing, too, even after Clarke skinned a fish with his teeth on TV! He later became her partner.

Meanwhile, Jacinda was going places in Parliament. Before long, she became Deputy Leader of the Labour Party. Then in 2017, just weeks before the election, she was made the party's leader.

She spoke to New Zealanders about ending poverty, improving women's working lives, free university education, and fighting climate change. "Let's do this!" she kept saying.

She quickly became very popular. TV and radio commentators talked about "Jacindamania". Some people complained she was "too girly" or should be starting a family, but Jacinda just ignored them, and got on with her work.

In the election, the Labour Party won several more seats. They joined with two other parties to form a government. Jacinda Kate Laurell Ardern was the third female Prime Minister of New Zealand, our youngest leader for 160 years.

Three months later, she and Clarke announced that they were expecting a baby. "You can't be a new mother and do a good job as Prime Minister," some people said. "This is why a young woman can't be a good politician."

But Jacinda kept working, and going places. She and Clarke travelled to England, where she wore a korowai, a Māori feathered cloak, to meet Queen Elizabeth. Prince Charles and Clarke talked about fishing.

Neve Te Aroha Ardern Gayford was born on 21 June 2018, during the festival of Matariki.

Auckland's Sky Tower was lit up to mark the little girl's birth. Presents arrived from all over the world. Clarke and Jacinda kept the handmade gifts, and passed others on to charity.

After six weeks, the Prime Minister went back to work. Now their whole family was going places. At the United Nations in New York, Neve sat on her father's lap while her mother spoke to world leaders. Politicians from many countries cooed over the tiny girl.

In New Zealand, Jacinda and her government worked on ways to reduce poverty, and help children. They searched for ways to fight climate change.

Her job means she is usually busy from early in the day till 10 pm or later. On Saturdays, she may open a fair, or speak at a charity event, or meet a group to discuss an issue. On Sundays, she prepares for the next week's meetings.

Sometimes she watches rugby league or cricket. When they can, she and Clarke take Neve for a walk. They play with her and read to her.

Jacinda gets to meet many people.

"She'll talk to anyone," says her Auntie Marie.

They discuss peace, climate change, women's rights, and ending poverty.

Sometimes, people are rude or angry. That's just part of being a Prime Minister. But some meetings are very special. In February 2018, Jacinda spent five days meeting people at Waitangi, where the famous Treaty was signed in 1840. She was the first Prime Minister to stay there for so long.

On 15 March 2019, a gunman killed many Muslim New Zealanders while they were praying at their mosques in Christchurch. Jacinda Ardern flew straight to the city. She put on a hijab, a Muslim headscarf, to show respect for the victims.

She told the world that the victims were all true New Zealanders. "We are one," she said. She began some of her speeches in Arabic.

Famous people, including world leaders, sent messages of sadness and sympathy.

A photo of Jacinda hugging a young Somali-born woman was shone onto the world's tallest building, the 828-metre-high Burj Khalifa in Dubai.

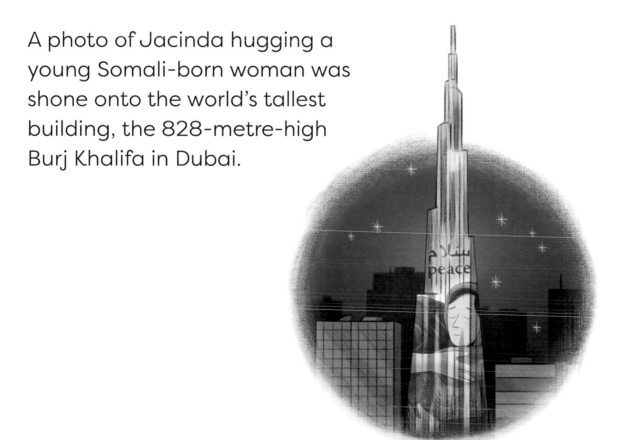

In 2019, the US magazine *Fortune* put Jacinda on its list of the world's greatest leaders.

She doesn't believe she is more special than any other working parent. "I'm a mother, not a Superwoman," she once said. But she hopes the things she's done might help everyone, especially girls, to believe they can also do things and go places.

Like New Zealand's young leader, they just have to get on with it.

1893
New Zealand women first in world to gain vote.

1918–1928
UK women gain vote.

1933
Elizabeth McCombs is New Zealand's first female MP.

1951
Tongan women gain vote.

1979
Margaret Thatcher is UK's first female Prime Minister.

1984
Ardern family moves to Murupara.

1990
Western Samoan women gain vote.

1997
Jenny Shipley is New Zealand's first female Prime Minister.

1999
Helen Clark is New Zealand's second female Prime Minister.

2005–2008
Jacinda in USA and UK. Works for British PM.

2001–2005
Jacinda works in the Beehive in Wellington.

1930
White South African women gain vote. (Black women cannot vote till 1994.)

1963
Fijian women gain vote.

1988
Ardern family moves to Morrinsville.

1997
Jacinda joins Labour Party.

2001
Jacinda graduates from University of Waikato, with Bachelor of Communication Studies degree.

1949
Iriaka Ratana is New Zealand's first female Māori MP.

1980 (26 JULY)
Jacinda Ardern born in Dinsdale, Hamilton.

1994
Jacinda attends Morrinsville College.

1999
General Election: Jacinda helps Labour Party campaign in New Plymouth.

1902
Australian women gain vote. (Aboriginal women cannot vote till 1962.)

1990
Dame Cath Tizard is New Zealand's first female Governor-General.

2010

Julia Gillard is Australia's first female Prime Minister.

2017 (25 FEBRUARY)

Jacinda elected MP for Mt Albert, Auckland.

2012–2014

Jacinda's DJ appearances.

2017 (1 MARCH)

Jacinda elected Deputy Leader of Labour Party.

2018 (19 JANUARY)

Jacinda and Clarke Gayford announce that they are expecting a baby.

2008

Jacinda elected President of International Union of Socialist Youth.

2011

Saudi Arabian women gain vote.

2016

Hillary Clinton campaigns to be President of the USA.

2018 (APRIL)

Jacinda attends Commonwealth Heads of Government meeting in London. Meets Queen Elizabeth II.

2019 (15 MARCH)

A gunman kills people at Christchurch mosques. Jacinda meets victims and their families.

2008 (8 NOVEMBER)

General Election: Jacinda enters New Zealand Parliament as Labour List MP.

2011

General Election: Jacinda stands for Auckland Central seat.

2013

Jacinda meets Clarke Gayford.

2017 (1 AUGUST)

Jacinda elected Labour Party Leader.

2017 (23 SEPTEMBER)

General Election.

2017 (26 OCTOBER)

Jacinda Ardern is New Zealand's third female Prime Minister.

2018 (21 JUNE)

Neve Te Aroha Ardern Gayford is born.

2018 (SEPTEMBER)

Jacinda speaks to United Nations General Assembly in New York.

2019 (APRIL)

Jacinda Ardern second on *Fortune* magazine's list of World's Greatest Leaders.

2014

General Election: Jacinda stands again for Auckland Central.